BMX'S

BY
Paul Estrem

EDITED BY
Howard Schroeder, Ph.D.
Professor in Reading and Language Arts
Dept. of Curriculum and Instruction
Mankato State University

PUBLISHED BY
CRESTWOOD HOUSE
Mankato, MN, U.S.A.

CIP

LIBRARY OF CONGRESS CATALOGING IN PUBLICATION DATA

Estrem, Paul.
  BMX's

(Super-charged!)
  SUMMARY: Introduces the sport of bicycle motocross, including the design of a BMX bike, riding and safety skills, and the features of a BMX racetrack.
  1. Bicycle motocross—Juvenile literature. [1. Bicycle motocross. 2. Bicycle, racing] I. Schroeder, Howard. II. Title.
  GV1049.3.E88   1987   796.6'2   87-15554
  ISBN 0-89686-349-2

International Standard Book Number:	Library of Congress Catalog Card Number:
0-89686-349-2	87-15554

CREDITS

Illustrations:
Cover Photo: John Ker/*BMX Plus!*
Mark Ahlstrom: 5, 14, 17, 18, 19, 21, 23, 26, 29, 30, 31, 33, 37
John Ker/*BMX Plus!*: 6-7, 9, 11, 24-25, 35, 39, 41, 42, 44-45
Su Kemper: 13
Graphic Design & Production:
Baker Street Productions, Ltd.
Technical Assistance:
Steven Jacobsen

Copyright© 1987 by Crestwood House, Inc. All rights reserved. No part of this book may be reproduced in any form without written permission from the publisher, except for brief passages included in a review. Printed in the United States of America.

Box 3427, Mankato, MN, U.S.A. 56002

TABLE OF CONTENTS

Introduction 4
The Exciting World of BMX 9
The Growing World of BMX 10
Why They're Called "BMX" Bikes 12
A Problem For Young Motocross Fans 14
How BMX Bikes Are Different 16
How BMX Freestylers Differ from Racers 28
Getting Ready 32
The Thrills of BMX Motocross Racing 38
The Thrills of BMX Freestyling 40
Is Organized BMX For You? 43
Glossary/Index 46-47

Special thanks to Don Doescher of
Scheel's Hardware & Sporting Goods (Mankato, MN)
for his help with the photographs in this book.

INTRODUCTION

Early Saturday morning, Dylan woke up to the smell of a wonderful aroma drifting down the hallway. Hot pancakes, eggs and bacon! He opened his eyes and yawned. Then he heard Mom, Dad and his little sister Erin in the kitchen. They were laughing and whispering.

Dylan threw back his covers and jumped out of bed. He looked over at the other side of the bedroom. There it was! His new BMX bike was propped against the wall under the window, just where he had put it last night. The morning sunlight sparkled on the chrome frame, and seemed to dance on the shiny spokes and reflectors. He smiled when he remembered polishing it and taking the kickstand off before going to bed.

The bike track! A shiver of excitement ran through Dylan when he remembered why he had taken the kickstand off. Today he was going to the BMX racetrack! Mom and Dad had given him his new bike on his birthday last Tuesday. They had also said they would take him and his friend, Ted, to the BMX track this morning. Dylan and Ted had never even seen the track before!

Dylan raced into the kitchen in his pajamas. His heart was beating wildly. "Mom, you better save me some of those pancakes—I don't want to get hungry at the track!" he cried. Mom, Dad and Erin were seated by the table. They were eating their breakfast with big smiles on their faces.

A BMX racer sits ready for speed and excitement.

"Sit down, son," Dad said. "Before you get any breakfast, you have something to open!" Mom and Erin laughed. Dylan looked down at the table. He saw a big gift-wrapped box by his place.

"Late Happy Birthday!" they all shouted. Dylan pulled his chair out and sat down. "Open it, open it!" Erin cried. "That's right," Mom said, "that's the only way you can make room for your breakfast."

Dylan smiled at his family as he untied a big red ribbon on the box. He quickly opened the box. A shiny black BMX helmet was inside, along with matching

A day at a BMX track is never dull!

gloves, elbow pads and knee pads.

"Wow!" Dylan exclaimed. "I thought my birthday was over! Thank you, thank you!" he cried as he ran around the table, giving his family lots of kisses. "Now I can ride like the pros at the track!"

The doorbell rang just as Dylan washed his last pancake down with a big drink of milk. "That's Ted!" he shouted, wiping his mouth with the back of his hand. He grabbed his new helmet, pulled it on and ran to the front door.

When Dylan opened the door, Ted greeted him with

a big grin and stuck both thumbs up in the air. Dylan could see Ted's red BMX "freestyler" with gray "mag" wheels leaning on the fence post behind him. Ted was wearing his helmet, gloves and pads.

"Neat helmet, Dylan!" Ted cried as he followed Dylan into the kitchen. "Great pajamas, too. Are you going to wear them to the track?"

"Ted's right, Dylan," Dad said. "You'd better get dressed so we can get to the track. Ted and I will put his bike in the station wagon while you get dressed. Mom and Erin—are you ready to go?"

Dylan quickly put his breakfast dishes in the sink and ran to his bedroom. He dressed, then brushed his teeth. Carefully, he wheeled his new bike down the hall, out the door and to the waiting car.

"Dad, aren't you going to bring your ten-speed, too?" Dylan teased. His dad smiled as he loaded Dylan's BMX into the back of the station wagon, next to Ted's bike.

"That's a good joke, Dylan," Dad chuckled. "I think you already know that my old touring bike wouldn't have a chance at the BMX track. Go get your mom and sister—then let's get out to the track!"

THE EXCITING WORLD OF BMX

If you're a BMX "old-timer," you can probably remember being as excited as Dylan and Ted on your first visit to an official BMX racetrack. Today, however, there are more reasons to be excited about BMX biking than ever before.

In fact, it doesn't matter if you have or haven't tried BMX biking. The many BMX bicycles, accessories and activities available today are thrilling for everyone!

The world of BMX has seen many changes in the past few years. For example, the first BMX bicycles were homemade. You couldn't just walk into a bike shop and ask for a BMX bike. There weren't any! Your choices were to "soup up" your own bike at home, or have someone do it for you. Today, bike stores offer many brands and styles of BMX bikes.

Bicycle companies didn't make BMX accessories in

Today there are thousands of BMX tracks throughout the world. Shown above is the Dixieland Raceway in Nashville, Tennessee.

the early days, either. If you wanted special handlebars or safety equipment, you had to build them yourself. BMX "pioneers" welded their own frames and handlebars. Many of them used football helmets and protective pads for safety.

The first BMX riders didn't have official tracks to race on. They had to search for racing areas. Today, there are thousands of tracks thoughout the world set aside for BMX racing. Many of these tracks are being improved and expanded to make them more challenging for the BMX racer.

THE GROWING WORLD OF BMX

Recently, BMX "freestyle" bikes have become very popular. Instead of racing, freestyle riders work on stunts, jumping, tight turns and handling tricks. BMX freestyle bikes and accessories are somewhat different than those used for racing. They must be built rugged enough to endure the stress of stunts and jumping.

If you have ever shopped for a BMX bike, you already know that there are many bikes and accessories from which to choose. The most important decision you will have to make is which BMX activity you enjoy most—racing or freestyle.

BMX freestyler Dizz Hicks does a kick turn on a small ramp.

WHY THEY'RE CALLED "BMX" BIKES

To understand how BMX bicycles first got their "BMX" name, you will need to know some facts about both bicycles and motorcycles.

Did you know that the first motorcycle was actually a bicycle with a motor attached to it? In fact, the words "motor" and "bicycle" were combined to make the word "motorcycle."

Until the late 1930's, the most popular motorcycles were large, heavy machines. They were designed to be driven on the road, not through muddy fields or over rough terrain. Their frames and motors were very large and heavy. Their wheels were almost as big as the tires on a pickup truck. In fact, tow trucks were sometimes needed to pull these motorcycles out of ditches!

Motorcycle companies soon began to build smaller, lighter, and faster machines. With lightweight frames and smaller tires, these motorcycles were easier to handle on the road. Drivers also found they could ride through mud, loose sand and gravel quite easily.

Cross-country motorcycle racing soon became popular with these lightweight machines. This new sport was named "motocross" by putting together the words "motorcycle" and "cross-country." The abbreviation for "motocross" is "MX."

Why are BMX bikes called "BMX" bikes? Because

"BMX" bicycle racing got its name from motocross (MX) motorcycle racing. Bicycle motocross is similar to motorcycle motocross in two ways:

First, BMX racetracks are planned and built much the same as motocross tracks. In both sports, a difficult cross-country course is mapped out through mud, loose sand, and gravel.

Second, BMX bicycles are compact, light, and rugged. They are built to stand up to hard riding on rough terrain. MX motorcycles are built in a similar way. There is one main difference between the two machines: the motorcycle is motor-powered and the bicycle is foot-powered.

Like MX motorcycles, BMX bikes are built for heavy-duty action.

A standard street bike (left) is not designed for off-road use. To the right is a BMX racer.

A PROBLEM FOR YOUNG MOTOCROSS FANS

Like many fads, motocross motorcycle racing first became popular on the West Coast. By the early 1960's, MX racing had become a popular spectator sport. Thousands of motocross fans went to the tracks for fun and excitement.

The popularity of motocross racing soon spread throughout the country. Many adult motocross fans bought their own MX motorcycles. They now had the freedom to actually experience the thrills of "dirt-bike" riding.

Young motocross fans didn't have the same freedom. First, many of them weren't old enough to drive. In most cases, they weren't big enough to handle a motorcycle. Finally, many couldn't afford to buy their own dirt bikes.

What did they do? They began to imitate their favorite motocross drivers on their standard street or touring bikes!

Young motocross fans soon discovered some disappointing facts about their standard bicycles. First, they were hard to ride in dirt-bike conditions. It was not easy to ride them fast through mud, sand, or gravel.

Second, they weren't built to take the stress of motocross tricks and stunts. Jumping, wheelies, and slides were very hard on most standard bikes. Young riders often walked their bikes home with flat tires, bent handlebars, missing spokes or broken forks. Parents everywhere saw a rapid increase in bicycle repair costs.

HOW BMX BIKES ARE DIFFERENT FROM OTHER BIKES

The first BMX bikes appeared in bicycle shops in the late 1960's. Bicycle companies had been watching young MX fans imitate motocross drivers on their standard bikes. They saw, and began to build, what the young riders wanted in a true motocross bicycle.

The following pages will help you better understand how BMX bikes are different from other bicycles.

Motocross Handlebars

A set of rugged, high-rise handlebars, with a connecting cross brace, is needed to withstand hard spills and slides. The best BMX handlebars are made from either a strong aluminum alloy or chrome-moly materials. An "alloy" is two or more metals mixed together. "Chrome-moly" is tempered chrome molybdenum, a strong, lightweight metal compound. The high position of the handles allows a firm grip with both hands while sitting or standing.

Special Handlebar Stem

Often called the "gooseneck," this piece is made of a clamp and shaft that holds the handlebars to the head tube. Because the bars are pushed, pulled, and jerked left and right during races and stunts, the gooseneck must not allow slipping or loosening. The best goosenecks are the double-clamp type held by four bolts. The

Most BMX bikes have high-rise handlebars with a double-clamp gooseneck.

shaft is usually made from a reinforced chrome-moly material.

Hand Brakes

In the past, most standard street bicycles were equipped with foot-controlled coaster brakes on the rear wheel. The rider pushed back on one of the pedals to slow down or stop.

Most BMX racing techniques and stunts require the use of both front and rear brakes while pedaling. Stand-

Hand-operated caliper brakes give the rider better control when racing or performing stunts.

ing on one pedal without braking is often necessary. For these reasons, dual hand-operated caliper brakes are used on most BMX bikes. Some racers and freestylers like to use rear coaster brakes for special events and tricks.

No Gearshift

Most BMX riding calls for short bursts of speed over a short distance. Endurance racing over a long distance is usually for full-size touring bikes. Professional BMX riders have found that shifting gears is not helpful during competition. In fact, a gearshift can actually get in the way of BMX handlebar control and hand-braking. Most BMX bikes do not have gearshifts.

Smaller Tires

In the early days, BMX pioneers found that the large twenty-four or twenty-six inch (61 or 66 cm) tires on their standard bikes couldn't hold up under BMX punishment. Also, the tires were too large to control in mud, loose sand or gravel. By experimenting, they also found that the sixteen-inch (41 cm) tires on "beginner" bikes were too small. They didn't provide the traction or the speed that was needed. BMXers finally used the twenty-inch (51 cm) tire size used on "mid-range" bicycles. Knobby tires are most often used in BMX racing events.

The twenty-inch (51 cm) tire (middle) offers the best speed and traction for BMX racing.

Reinforced Wheel Rims

In both racing and freestyling, BMX bike wheels take a beating. Two types of wheel rims are popular: spoke rims and "mag" wheels. BMX spoke rims are built to be more rugged than those used on standard bikes. Most BMX rims have thirty-two or thirty-six spokes—more than the twenty-eight spokes usually found on standard bike wheels. Also, the spokes on a BMX wheel are built from stronger materials. Spoke rims are often made of steel or alloyed aluminum.

"Mag" wheels are one-piece BMX bike wheels made from aluminum alloy or reinforced plastic materials. They do not have spokes and are more durable than spoked wheels. However, they are heavier. Because both spoke and mag-wheel types are popular in BMX racing and freestyling, wheel selection is mostly based on what the rider likes best.

Reinforced Front Fork

The front forks on most standard bikes are not made for rough front-wheel handling. A few BMX jumps, turns, "wheelies" or "endo's" could damage or destroy the front fork. (An "endo" is like a wheelie, only you raise the rear wheel up in the air by bumping the front wheel against a curb or other object.) A BMX front fork needs to be tough, and is usually made of chrome-moly steel. Most BMX front forks have an axle "drop-out" for quick front wheel removal.

Smaller, More Durable Frame

A BMX bike frame must be very strong to withstand stress. The frame consists of a top tube, down tube, seat tube, two seat stays, and two chain stays. Metal braces are often added for extra support. Most BMX frames are built small to allow longer pedal cranks and provide more clearance from the ground. Frames are most often built from reinforced aluminum alloy or chrome-moly. Like the front forks, most BMX frames have a rear axle "drop-out" for quick rear wheel removal.

Most BMX bikes have rear axle "drop-outs" for faster tire changes.

Extended Seat Post

Tall BMXers ride the same size bikes as short BMXers. A strong, extra-long seat post lets tall riders adjust the seat higher. Each BMX rider knows what's best for him.

Racing Saddle

Most competitive BMX riding is done standing up on the pedals. In this way, the rider can put maximum "push power" (torque) on the pedals. Seating comfort during racing is not a major concern. The most popular BMX seat is the same narrow, hard seat used on full-size racing bikes.

Drivetrain

The BMX bicycle drivetrain includes the front sprocket, chain, and rear sprocket. The sizes of the front and rear sprockets determine whether a bike is built for power or for speed. A large front sprocket and small rear sprocket are best for high speed on a flat track. A small front sprocket and a large rear sprocket are best for getting the power needed to climb a hill or for a freestyle stunt.

On some BMX bikes, the front sprocket cannot be removed from the crank set. The whole crank set must be replaced in order to change to a larger or smaller front sprocket. On other BMX bikes, a front sprocket "spider" can be easily removed and replaced. The removable spider is a star-shaped sprocket that is bolted to the crank set.

Above are two front sprockets. The black one (bottom) has forty-one teeth and the white one (top) has forty-four teeth.

Crank Set & Pedals

BMX bikes often come with longer pedal cranks than standard bikes. This gives them more torque (pedal power) for fast acceleration. BMX cranks are built tough to take the heavy stress of BMX competition.

The most popular foot pedal used on BMX bikes is the standard "rat trap." The pedal surface is often fitted with nonskid teeth or ridges for gripping power. The toe clips used on full-sized racers should never be used

BMX racers round a curve at Chandler, Arizona.

BMX bikes don't have fenders or chainguards.

on BMX bikes. BMX racing and stunts demand free foot action between the pedal and the ground.

No Fenders

Many standard street bikes have fenders on both wheels. The main reason for fenders is to keep water, mud and dirt off the rider. On a BMX bike, fenders add weight and could even get in the way. And most BMX riders don't really care about getting dirty. If fenders are used at all, they're small, lightweight and mostly for looks.

No Chainguard

On a standard bicycle, a chainguard has several functions. First, it keeps the rider from getting splattered in bad weather. It also helps keep the rider's trousers from getting caught in the chain and front sprocket. In addition, it protects the chain itself from the rider's feet.

Most BMXers do not use chainguards. They want to have quick access to the chain if it falls off or breaks. Their tight-fitting BMX riding pants seldom get caught in the chain. Also remember that most BMXers don't really care about getting muddied up!

No Kickstand

Most BMX bicycles are sold with kickstands installed. But the kickstands are always removed during BMX racing or freestyling events. In day-to-day riding, BMXers must decide for themselves whether or not to use the kickstand.

Protective Pads

BMX bicycle handlebars and top tubes are usually wrapped with nylon-covered pads made of thick foam. Pads should always be in place during competition. Helmets, elbow and knee pads, and other protective equipment should also be worn during BMX activities.

HOW BMX FREESTYLERS DIFFER FROM BMX RACERS

Recently, the BMX world began to include "freestyling" as well as motocross racing. This can be confusing when you are shopping for a bike or accessories. You will have to know what you want.

Your first job is to ask yourself this question: "Do I want to mostly race or freestyle with my BMX bike?" When you are thinking it over, remember that BMX racing and stunt bikes—and their accessories—are somewhat different. Also remember that both are similar in many ways. You will be able to compromise.

The following pages will help you better understand the differences between BMX "dirt bikes" (for racing) and "street bikes" (for freestyling).

Freestyle Handlebars—Most BMX racing handlebars are bent back slightly at the handles. This provides the best gripping angle for cross-country riding. Most freestyle handlebars, however, are not bent back and have a straight crossbar across the top. This straight crossbar is needed to perform various riding stunts.

Freestyle Goosenecks—At first glance, BMX goosenecks look the same. But, there can be at least two important differences: First, freestyle goosenecks may have a special "stepping" platform for stunts. Second, some freestyle bikes have a special gooseneck "rotor" mechanism. This rotor lets the rider spin the front wheel and handlebars without twisting or breaking the front brake cable.

Freestyle Brakes—Most BMX riders prefer hand-operated caliper brakes for both wheels. Some professional riders—both racers and tricksters—prefer foot-controlled coaster brakes in back with hand brakes in front. The rear brake calipers on racers are most often attached near the seat stays. The rear brake calipers on freestyle bikes are sometimes mounted lower, close to the chain stays. Why? If a rear top tube platform is used, the rear calipers must be mounted out of the way in a lower position.

This rotor system allows a freestyler to spin the fork without breaking the brake cable.

Freestyle Tires & Rims—Except for "junior" models and special "trick" bikes, twenty-inch (51 cm) tires are used on most BMX freestyle bikes. Dirt bikes most often have "knobby" tires for traction. Freestylers and indoor racers most often use smoother tires for better traction on paved surfaces.

Many BMX racers like to use spoke rims since they are lighter. Freestylers often use mags since they stand up better. Some freestylers like to use spoke rims covered with colorful plastic hubs.

Freestyle Frames—Both racing and freestyle BMX frames are made to withstand heavy stress. Freestyle frames are often equipped with "extras" to aid stunt performance. Stepping platforms can be added to the top tube, seat stays and chain stays. Flip-down standing pegs can also be mounted on the chain stays. Dual top tubes and special braces are often used for platform support.

The BMX racer tire (left) is knobbier than the freestyle tire (right).

Freestyle Front Forks—The front-fork tubes on a BMX freestyle bike can have either built-in standing platforms or flip-down standing pegs.

Freestyle Saddles—Most BMX racers use the same narrow, hard seat used on full-size racing bikes. Freestyle riders sometimes use saddles that swivel and turn to help them perform tricks and stunts.

Freestyle Pedals—To get the most "pedal power," most BMX freestylers use the same long pedal cranks as BMX racers. Almost all BMX racing bikes use "rat-trap" foot pedals. Many freestylers use "rat-trap" pedals, but some like to use larger "bear-trap" foot pedals for tricks and stunts.

Freestyle Gearshifts—Most BMX racing and freestyle bikes do not have gearshifts. Some professional freestylers have been known to use them for special tricks and stunts, however.

Pegs on a freestyler's front fork are used to stand on during stunts.

GETTING READY— THE BMX BASICS

It's a big thrill to get your first BMX bike. The first urge is to hop on, stomp down on the pedals and try a wheelie. At this point, it is wise to stop and think about this: The best riders spent many hours practicing in order to learn their skills. Some of them ignored the BMX "basics" and learned the hard way!

You will enjoy riding most if you remember some riding and safety "basics." This is true for organized racing, freestyling, or just riding down the street to a friend's house.

Your BMX bike is built to take a lot of punishment. But it has weaknesses, too. It's important to know what those weaknesses are. The BMX "basics" are important for another reason. You should understand them in order to protect both yourself and others. You should think about the following BMX "basics" whenever you get ready to ride your bike.

Clothing

You should always wear proper clothes when you ride your bike. This is important for both comfort and safety. It is a good idea to know what you're going to do on your bike before you go.

Are you going out to run a quick errand? Your regular or school clothes will be fine in good weather. But you will have to remember not to try anything fancy! Are

Wearing laced shoes and pants that are tight around the ankles can prevent a spill.

you going to spend the morning exploring a wild off-the-road area with some friends? It would be smart to wear old, worn play clothes. You will most likely take a few spills. Are you going to practice freestyling at the playground? Loose-fitting clothes will be the easiest to move around in.

Durable long-sleeved shirts and trousers are always best for your safety. If you take a spill, you will have a better chance of not getting cuts and bruises. Shirts should be loose enough to give your arms freedom of movement. Trousers should be tight in the legs so they won't get caught in the chain.

What about shoes and socks? For most day-to-day

casual riding, your favorite tennis shoes will be fine. Just be sure that the soles grip the pedals well. For heavy racing or freestyling, you should select your footwear more carefully. Lacing is important so your shoes don't fall off during a race or stunt. You will probably want to protect your ankles with heavy socks and high-top shoes during a race. You should always select lightweight shoes for BMX racing or freestyling.

Special BMX Protective Gear

Selecting the right riding clothes is important. Using special BMX protective gear is even more important. BMX biking is a rough-and-tumble sport. The best way to be prepared for a spill is to use safety gear at all times.

Head and face injuries can be the most serious. A good helmet and a face protector are very important. Always wear your helmet, even on short trips down the block.

Most competitions require that you wear special BMX gloves, elbow pads, knee pads and shoulder pads. You should also wear them during practice.

You can find special BMX riding pants, shirts, jackets and one-piece suits at most bicycle shops. They are lightweight, rugged, and provide a lot of comfort and protection. Most of them have built-in protective pads.

Although you don't really wear them, the protective pads on your handlebars, gooseneck and top tube are important safety features. The pads are made to prevent face and body injuries. They're required in many BMX competitions and should be on at all times.

Proper safety gear is important—no matter what kind of stunts you are doing!

Safety Check!
Before riding, you should always check over your bike. You can avoid many problems by using the simple ten-point checklist below. And remember, if you don't know how to adjust or fix a part, don't try to do it yourself!
 1. Check handlebars and gooseneck for position and tightness. Check protective pads on handlebars, gooseneck and top tube.
 2. Check front and rear brake levers and calipers.
 3. Check frame, front fork and special equipment (platforms, pegs, rotor, etc.).
 4. Check wheel alignment and tightness.
 5. Check spoke condition and tire pressure.
 6. Check condition and tightness of sprockets, cranks and pedals.
 7. Check chain condition and tension.
 8. Check seat position and tightness.
 9. Check condition and cleanliness of all reflectors.
 10. Check all bolts and fasteners for tightness.
 And don't forget: If you're going to park your bike, be sure that you have a strong bike lock!

Rules of the Road
It's time to hit the road. And whether you're racing, freestyling or just riding around the neighborhood, the same rules of the road apply:
• Ask your local police department about bicycle license requirements. Also ask for a bike-riding rule book. Read the rules and obey them!

The chain tension should "give" a bit.

- Never "ride" or "buck" a passenger on your bike. It's dangerous and illegal.
- Always ride "with" traffic on the right side of the road. Stay close to the curb, but watch for opening car doors. Also watch for cars pulling into traffic. Always ride carefully.
- Watch for drain grates, potholes, slippery spots and other obstructions.
- Always yield to other vehicles and be polite to pedestrians. Use hand signals for stops and turns.
- Always use extra caution at night or in bad weather.
- Always keep both hands on the handlebars in traffic.

And remember: Save all your BMX stunts for the driveway, track, or freestyle area!

THE THRILLS OF BMX MOTOCROSS RACING

There's nothing quite like a pack of BMX "moto" racers in an intense dirt-bike competition. One main difference separates motocross motorcycle and BMX racing: In a BMX race, there's no loud engine noise—just the huffing and puffing of hard-pedaling bikers!

The key to all the excitement of BMX racing is the track itself. Let's look at some of the features of a typical BMX racetrack.

The Starting Gate—BMX tracks are usually wide enough to handle six or eight bikes at a time. On most tracks, the action starts at an electronic starting gate on the slope of a hill. The gate drops flat at the start of the race and the riders get a fast start down the hill.

Tabletop Jumps—This type of jump has a flat top with a sharp drop-off at the far end.

High Jump—Pileups often occur at the bottom of these jumps.

Water & Mud Jumps—You're a mess if you miss!

Bunny Hops—These low bumps will put you into a slide if you hit them too fast.

Whoop-de-do's—These rippling series of higher bumps are great for wheelies.

Berms—These fast turns are banked to the inside.

Flat Turns—These turns are not banked. It's easy to slide out if you're going too fast.

BMX racing action begins at an electronic starting gate on the slope of a hill.

The Final Stretch—A short straightaway can give those behind that last burst of speed before the checkered flag.

THE THRILLS OF BMX FREESTYLING

BMX freestyling can be as exciting to watch as a rough-and-tumble dirt-track race. Like automobile stunt driving, speed is not very important in freestyling. Daring stunts and tricky moves provide the excitement. Let's take a look at some of the more spectacular BMX freestyle stunts.

Wheelie—This basic freestyle maneuver is used by both racers and freestylers. Get the front end up and see how long you can last on the rear wheel!

Endo—This trick is usually performed by bumping into a curb or other low obstruction. See how high up you can get your rear wheel without crashing.

Flying—This trick is also called "taking air." How long can you stay airborne after a jump?

Kickturn—You'll need a ramp for this one. Ride to the top, do a wheelie, turn your bike around and ride back down. Sounds simple? It isn't.

Ramping—After getting your kickturn down, you can learn ramp rollbacks, jumps, endo's and spins.

Free-Form—Like professional breakdancing, a creative freestyler in top form is great to watch. Here's where you'll see stepping pegs and platforms used.

Endo!

"Mom, Dad, Erin!" Dylan cried as he slid his dusty bike to a stop behind their parked car. "I qualified, I qualified! I'm in the beginner's race next Saturday! Ted's going to be in the freestyle competition, too!" Dylan's family cheered as Mr. Larson, the qualifying judge, walked up to them.

"You have a fine beginning BMX racer here, folks," Mr. Larson said with a smile as he looked at Dylan. "We're looking forward to seeing both Dylan and Ted here next Saturday. In fact, we hope they will both be able to come down here often in the future."

These whoop-de-do's are sure to cause a few spills.

"We'll all be here next weekend," Dylan's dad said as he shook Mr. Larson's hand. "We didn't know how exciting this was going to be. Thanks for everything!"

As Mr. Larson turned to walk back to the track, he saw Ted flash past him, doing a wheelie. At the last second, Ted tried an endo on the curb. He bounced onto the boulevard instead. Luckily, both Ted and his bike landed unhurt.

Ted looked embarrassed when he took off his helmet and smiled at all of them from the grass. They all laughed when Dylan exclaimed, "Neat crash-and-burn, Ted. It's time to get home to practice those endo's. No lunch for you today!"

IS ORGANIZED BMX FOR YOU?

Like Dylan and Ted, maybe you're just getting started in the world of BMX riding. Or, maybe you've been riding for a while but have never seen or participated in an official BMX competition. How can you learn more?

The quickest way to learn more is to visit a BMX track or event like Dylan and Ted. You will be able to meet lots of people who love BMX and know a lot about it. They will be happy to tell you how to get involved.

Another way is to talk to your nearest BMX bicycle dealer. Bike dealers will gladly tell you about BMX groups and events in your area. They can also tell you how to get BMX newsletters and magazines. This will

Whether you choose racing or freestyling, the world of BMX is always a lot of fun!

help you contact national BMX organizations and keep up with the latest developments in the world of BMX.

Whatever you decide to do with your BMX bike, remember that there's a big BMX world out there, just waiting for you!

GLOSSARY / INDEX

ACCESSORIES 6, 7, 9, 10, 27, 28, 30, 34 — *Extra or special equipment, such as helmets, gloves, or stepping platforms.*

ALLOY 16, 20, 21 — *Two or more metals mixed together.*

BERM 38 — *A fast turn banked to the inside.*

BMX 4, 5, 6, 8, 9, 10, 12, 13, 16, 17, 18, 19, 20, 21, 22, 23, 26, 27, 28, 29, 30, 31, 32, 34, 37, 38, 40, 42, 43, 44, 45 — *Abbreviation for "bicycle motocross."*

BUNNY HOP 38 — *Series of low bumps on a track.*

CALIPER BRAKES 18, 29, 36 — *Hand-controlled brakes that grip the front or rear wheel rim with a squeezing action.*

CHROME-MOLY 16, 17, 20, 21 — *Tempered chrome molybdenum, a strong, lightweight metal compound.*

COASTER BRAKES 18, 29 — *Pedal-controlled brakes that grip the hub of the rear wheel.*

DIRT BIKE 15, 28, 30, 38 — *BMX bike equipped specifically for BMX motocross racing.*

DROP-OUT 20, 21 — *An axle connecting piece that provides easy removal and replacement of front or rear wheels.*

ENDO 20, 40, 41, 43 — *Pushing down on the handlebars, leaning forward and raising the rear wheel up off the ground. A reverse wheelie.*

MOTOCROSS 12, 13, 14, 15, 16, 28, 38 — *Cross-country motorcycle racing, after which BMX bicycle racing is patterned.*

MX 12, 13, 14, 15, 16 — *Abbreviation for "motorcycle motocross."*

RAMPING 40 — *Performing freestyle stunts such as kickturns, rollbacks, jumps, endo's and spins on a steep ramp.*

STREET BIKE 15, 26, 28 — *BMX bike equipped specifically for BMX "freestyling" (stunts, jumping, tricks).*

TABLETOP 38 — *A flat-topped jump with a sharp drop-off at the far end.*

TAKING AIR 40 — *Staying airborne as long as possible after a jump. Also called "flying."*

TORQUE 22, 23 — *Amount of force used, as in pedaling.*

TRACTION 30 — *Gripping power, as in tire treads gripping the pavement.*

WHEELIE 15, 20, 32, 38, 40, 43 — *Pulling back on the handlebars, raising the front wheel up and riding only on the rear wheel.*

WHOOP-DE-DO 38, 42 — *A rippling series of high bumps on a track.*

Ce volume,
le trois cent quatre-vingt-onzième
de la collection Poésie,
a été composé par Interligne et
achevé d'imprimer sur les presses
de Bussière Camedan Imprimeries à Saint-Amand (Cher),
le 16 mars 2004.
Dépôt légal : mars 2004.
Numéro d'imprimeur : 041328/1.

ISBN 2-07-031399-9./Imprimé en France.

128034